An Introduction to

Basic Supervision of People

This book is in the

ADDISON-WESLEY Series in

Supervisory Training

An Introduction to
Basic Supervision
of People

by

RAYMOND J. BURBY

Douglas Aircraft Company, Inc.
Long Beach, California

ADDISON-WESLEY PUBLISHING COMPANY, INC.
Reading, Massachusetts
Palo Alto · London · Don Mills, Ontario

This book is also available in editions in the following languages:

Dutch
Japanese
Spanish

Third printing, April 1972

ACKNOWLEDGMENT

Almost any endeavor is the result of some sort of motivation. In my case, it was the result of an afternoon's conversation with Bert Holtby, to whom I am deeply indebted. He carried me past the inspiration of thinking about something to doing it.

Preface

This material on supervision has been programed to be a self-teaching book. Its purpose is to take you through the course one step at a time. As you follow along you will find that you are given many opportunities to prove to yourself that you are learning and getting an increasingly better understanding of the subject.

Our book differs from conventional textbooks in that it is in a form usually referred to as a "scramble book." This means simply that if you select one answer to a question you proceed to one page, and if you select a different answer you go to another. If your answer is right, you'll be told to go on to a new topic. If it is wrong, you'll be told to go back and select another answer. All this involves, of course, a certain amount of skipping around. However, at the top of each answer page you will find in parentheses the number of the page on which the question appeared.

Before you start this course, we suggest that you take the Pre-Test which you will find at the back of the book. After completing the course you will do this same test again as a Post-Test. Then you can score yourself by checking your answers with those provided at the back of the book. You will also be able to measure how much you have learned by comparing your own two sets of answers.

Long Beach, California
November, 1965   R.J.B.

Contents

CHAPTER 1

Introduction

This course is designed primarily for the first-line supervisor. If it is your job to direct other people, you are a supervisor. You are a first-line supervisor if the people you direct do not, in turn, direct other people. The purpose of this course is to expose you to basic principles that will help you develop your talent for supervising people. Naturally, you cannot expect a course of study as condensed as this to solve all your problems in dealing with people. What it can do, however, is direct your attention to the skills you must have or develop in order to be a good supervisor. Your ability to acquire or improve these skills will require diligent practice in your day-to-day relationships with the workers who look to you for direction.

The material you are going to study does not deal with specialized job knowledge, paperwork routine, or similar activities. We take it for granted that you are familiar with the work and know your organization and its particular procedures. In fact, your knowledge about machines, schedules, costs, planning, safety regulations, and so forth was no doubt the reason you were made a supervisor. It may be that you are still being trained and instructed in these areas in accordance with your organization's specific needs. But in addition, a new dimension has been added to your responsibilities — you are now directing other people. Before this, as a skilled worker, you were given responsibilities — now you must delegate them.

1

Fortunately, the basic skills needed in supervising people are the same regardless of the specific jobs to be done or the varying employee skills that are involved. Whether you are concerned with airplanes or roller skates, insurance or social work, skilled or unskilled workers, whatever you learn from this study will be of use. When you become familiar with the fundamental principles in this course and acquire skill in applying them, your abilities as a supervisor can grow to keep pace, not only with your present position, but wherever your talents and fate may place you in the future.

Whether you have assumed your first-line supervisory job as a new employee or as an "old hand" is of little consequence. Your background, that particular mixture of reason and experience you bring to the job, is

as individual as your finger-
prints. This course of study
is designed to provide a frame-
work on which to build your
skill as a supervisor. Your
past experience may make it
easier for you to absorb and
apply the ideas you find in
this course, but any lack of
experience need not hinder your progress if you understand and practice the material it contains.

In this study you are going to be exposed to the following areas of supervisory know-how:

Basic reasons people work	Leadership traits
	Training and motivation
How people differ	Principles for good job relations
How people learn	
Basic supervisory skills	Communicating
	Job standards
The decision-making process	Safety

After completing the course, you will be tested. A
grade of 90 or more will demonstrate your understanding of these principles. Furthermore, the results should prove to you that you have become familiar
with what will be required of you as a skilled supervisor. It is important that you recognize various
concepts and learn how to use them. Any one of them
could become the subject for a deep, detailed study.
You can find whole books devoted to one or more of the
topics listed above. It would be wise, after completing

this course, to see what
your local library might
have on hand and, on your
own initiative, to search
out material in those areas
which you feel will increase
your individual capability
as a supervisor.

Much of the material is presented in a way which tests
your understanding of what you have studied. This
program is designed to give you a very broad picture
of what is involved in supervising people. You will
not be asked to memorize everything. Certain key
points, however, you should remember. You will find
these points emphasized several times.

Do not hesitate to take notes. Not only can notes help
you memorize an important subject or thought, but
they may serve to stress areas where you need more
improvement or deeper study. You will find working
your way through this material very interesting. It will
require that you understand the point being stressed,
and it will give you an opportunity to practice your
understanding.

First you must understand and become familiar with
a principle, then you must put that principle to work.
The first requires knowledge, the second, skill. For
this reason, the material in this course is not presented in the usual manner. You will often find a para-
graph or two which discusses a specific subject. You
will be questioned about your understanding of the material. You will select the best answer from several
choices provided. A page reference accompanies each

choice, and you will turn to the page indicated for the answer you select. If your answer is correct, you will be so informed and will go on to new material. If your answer is incorrect, you will be sent back to the question page to make another selection. Using the program is like having a teacher beside you as you study.

Take your time. What you learn in these pages can be of great importance to you.

CHAPTER 2

Understanding People

Most people work to make enough money for the necessities and some of the luxuries of life. This is quite an elementary observation. There are, however, many other reasons why people work. We must go a little deeper into these less obvious reasons for their taking and keeping a job. In other words, what we need to know is what <u>motivates</u> people.

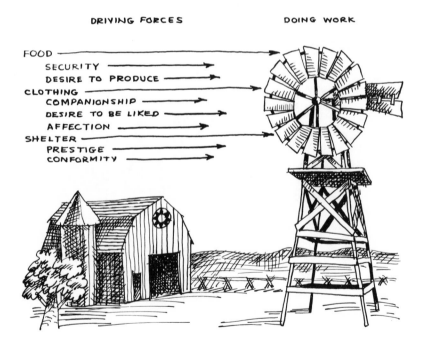

6

From the following four choices, select the answer that you feel most completely describes the basic reasons why people work. Then turn to the page that is indicated beside the answer you have chosen.

1. Companionship
   Desire to produce
   Desire to be liked...................... Page 9

2. Affection
   Prestige
   Conformity........................... Page 10

3. Food
   Clothing
   Shelter
   Security .... Page 11

4. All of these .... Page 12

You didn't follow instructions!

You are probably so used to turning to the next page while reading a book that you quite naturally did it again this time. But the material in this book is not organized that way. Instead, each time you answer a question you should proceed directly to the page that is indicated beside your answer.

▶ Please return to page 7 and read the instructions again.

(from page 7)

You selected group 1.

    Companionship
    Desire to produce
    Desire to be liked

Certainly, these are some of the basic reasons for working. But does this list account completely for why we work? Some of the other reasons listed are just as basic.

▶ Please return and select a better answer.

You selected group 2.

    Affection
    Prestige
    Conformity

Yes, these are some of the basic reasons for working, but they are no more important than some of the other reasons that were listed.

▶ Please return and select a better answer.

You selected group 3.

Food
Clothing
Shelter
Security

This isn't the answer we were looking for.

It's true, as we said, that most people work so that they can make enough money to pay their bills. Perhaps you feel that by adding "security" to "food, clothing, and shelter" we have formed a complete list of the reasons for working.

Well, we agree that this group seems to be more urgent than the others. You could even say that these are the main reasons for working. But if you think about it, you'll agree that to be complete, our list should include some less obvious but equally basic reasons.

▶ Please return and select a better answer.

Your answer was 4. All of these.

Very good. You observed that no single one of the lists gave all the basic reasons for working. The entire list is repeated here for your review:

Food	Companionship
Clothing	Desire to be liked
Shelter	Affection
Security	Prestige
Desire to produce	Conformity

You will find that each person working for you is motivated by not one, but a combination of these factors. What is most important to one person may be of comparatively little importance to another. Part of your job is to learn to look for and to recognize the factors which motivate your workers.

We have given quite a long list of separate reasons why people work. Each of these may be easier to understand if we think in terms of the three fundamental drives which motivate people. These three drives are (1) to survive, (2) to reproduce one's own kind, and (3) to win personal recognition and appreciation. With a little thought, we can probably relate a person's desire for money, for affection, for prestige, etc., to one or another of these drives. Let's consider an example.

Mary is a new employee in the sales department, and her family depends heavily upon her income. She is a stenotypist who also must keep up the correspondence files. Because she decided to revise the filing system, Mary is behind schedule in her work. Every

one in the department had helped to teach her the
ropes and Bill, her supervisor, was understanding
and patient. But shortly after Mary was hired, Bill
was transferred to a branch office. Her new boss,
Al, is demanding and belittling. He bawls Mary out
in front of others, and shakes up the whole department. Mary is close to a breakdown.

Now, how do you explain Al's behavior in his new
job? From which of the following general needs does
it stem?

Your answer was 1. The need to survive.

This is not the best answer. Perhaps Al's demanding ways are due to fear of losing his job, but we doubt it. It would seem more likely that Al is looking for attention. He seems to want the people in the department to <u>know</u> he is the boss.

▶ Please return and choose a better answer.

You selected 2. The need to reproduce his own kind. This is not the most likely reason for Al's demanding behavior. Perhaps Al may appear to be manly by his domineering ways. On the other hand, his treatment of Mary could hardly be expected to make him attractive to the opposite sex. Ask yourself, "Is Al trying to let the workers know who is boss?" If this is what Al is doing, what is he really seeking?

▶ Please return and select a better answer.

3. The need to win recognition and appreciation.

You are correct. Al wants attention and respect from the office help, and his approach is to be demanding.

How about Mary? Why do you think she is headed for a breakdown? Which of these factors is most responsible?

You chose 1. The need for money (survival).

 Surely the best answer. You are coming along fine! Mary's family depends heavily upon her, and it's ten to one that feelings of insecurity outweigh any other feelings she may have about herself and her job. While it's true that some girls take certain jobs because they are looking for husbands, this does not seem to be the case here. Being upbraided and belittled by the boss probably makes Mary feel that she is on the verge of being fired.

Before leaving the subject of motivation, we should think about the reasons people work and their drives from another point of view. Most of the people working on the job are valuable assets to the business. The company wants to avoid losing the workers because they have become familiar with the company's way of doing things. Someone has had to spend time explaining procedures to the new workers and would have to go through the whole process once again if the worker should quit or be fired. Furthermore, no new replacement is up to his best performance until he is trained and the company's procedures have become routine. With this in mind, let's briefly explore one final example in this area of motivation.

Joe is an excellent tool and die maker. A new foundry is starting up close to his neighborhood and Joe is offered a job by one of the owners. Joe is told that the foundry's tool room is just getting under way, and that his chances of growing with the business are excellent. Joe's present job is satisfactory, but he is one of a group of twenty tool and die makers working for a large concern.

Joe tells his foreman about the job offer and the foreman says,

> "If you take it, you're crazy — that place might fold up tomorrow."

Joe isn't persuaded by this argument, and accepts the new job. The business doesn't fold. In fact, it slowly expands, and soon the toolroom has five die sinkers with Joe the acknowledged foreman.

However, the owner who hired Joe and who is managing the business begins to discuss some of the tooling problems with the other men. Joe resents this — he feels that he hasn't been treated fairly, and soon quits.

Here is a case study of a skilled man whom two companies employed but failed to hold. Why?

Some possible reasons are:

(a) His first foreman should have given Joe a better understanding of why he should stay with the larger concern.

(b) Joe is unstable.

(c) The owner of the small foundry didn't live up to his agreement.

(d) The large concern did not train its foreman in how to tell employees about company benefits.

(e) The owner of the small foundry failed to keep Joe posted on tooling problems.

Of these reasons, which do you think best apply to Joe's case?

1. (a), (b), and (c)......................Page 22

2. (a), (d), and (e)......................Page 23

3. (c), (d), and (e)......................Page 24

You answered 2. The need for a husband (reproduction).

This is incorrect. We do not even know from the case history given here whether Mary is single or married, and we have no indication that she's looking for a husband. We do know that she got along all right with her old boss, Bill. So we feel this is not a good answer.

▶ Please return and find a better answer.

You answered 3. The need to belong to the group. This is not the right answer. Mary has the help of everyone else in the department. They do not exclude her. It is more likely that she is concerned about her heavy family obligations.

▶ Please return and find the right answer.

You answered 1. (a), (b), and (c).

You are only partly right. We agree that Joe's first foreman could have made better and stronger appeals to Joe for staying on the job. He took a negative attitude, mentioning only the risk involved in changing to a newer, smaller company. After all, Joe is an excellent man at his job, he seems to be ambitious, and we doubt that he worried particularly about being able to earn a living. But if you think Joe is unstable because he left two jobs, you are putting the cart before the horse, confusing the cause and effect. Nothing about this case indicates that Joe is unstable.

We think that the owner of the new business did live up to his agreement with Joe. If a problem existed here, it was one of communication. Joe and the owner hadn't worked out a way to cover the handling of tooling problems.

▶ Please return to page 19. You can find a better answer.

You answered 2. (a), (d), and (e).

 You are correct. The foreman of the large concern could have answered Joe's reasons for leaving by emphasizing the many advantages of Joe's staying put, and by making a stronger appeal to his fundamental drive for recognition. The owner of the foundry did live up to his agreement, but he failed to keep Joe posted, or at least to get Joe's cooperation in discussing problems with the men. There was nothing wrong with discussing problems with any of the employees so long as Joe was in the communications channel. The owner's failure to keep Joe posted frustrated Joe's need for recognition and appreciation.

Let's think for a while about individual differences. People differ in looks, learning speeds, personality, and in many other ways. Just to test yourself on how you feel about individual differences, suppose you own a farm and raise berries. It is time to pick the berries and you need a man to help. Two men are available. One gives the impression of being slow and one looks as though he'd be quick. Which man would you choose?

1. The one who appears to be slow .... Page 25

2. The one who appears to be quick .... Page 26

You answered 3. (c), (d), and (e).

This is only partially correct.

You are right when you feel that the large concern should train the foremen to tell employees about the advantages of staying with the company. You are also correct in recognizing the problem Joe had with being bypassed by the owner of the foundry. However, the foundry owner did live up to his agreement with Joe. Joe was the foreman of the tool room as promised. The problem here seems to be one of communication between Joe and the owner.

▶ Please return and choose another answer.

Your answer was 1. The one who appears to be slow.

This is as good an answer as the other one. But of course neither answer is very good. Appearance has little or nothing to do with a person's capabilities.

We hope you made this choice because you suspected it was a poor question and you wondered what we would say. Well, all we can say is that looks have nothing to do with ability or brains.

▶ Please continue on page 27.

Your answer was 2. The one who appears to be quick.

If you selected the quick-looking person because you felt that he would naturally be more of an asset, your reason was not a sound one. We hope instead, that you said to yourself, "Neither selection is good, but I might as well make this one even though a person's looks has nothing to do with his capabilities." If so, you are on the right track.

The point, of course, is that looks and appearances can be deceptive, and facts simply do not support the opinion that a person who appears to be quick is any better than one who appears to be slow.

▶ Please go to page 27.

You may be saying to yourself, "that last question was unfair, since neither choice was really right." Well, all we wanted to put across was this one rule: <u>Please don't judge people's abilities by their looks</u>!

It is easy to jump to conclusions and put your fellow worker in some special category, to put him in a slot, so to speak. We have variations, then, not only among our workers, but in the way we as individuals see them and evaluate them. It is, of course, more difficult for a supervisor to understand workers who come from a background different from his own, but he should make every effort to do so. A good supervisor must understand himself well enough to make allowances for his own tendencies. The fact is there are usually several reasons why <u>we</u> think as we do about the people we meet, and <u>others</u> think differently.

This brings us back to individual differences. People don't <u>look</u> alike, they don't <u>act</u> alike, and they don't have <u>the</u> same <u>skills</u>. Here is a list of some of the ways people differ. You might want to make a copy of this list for future reference.

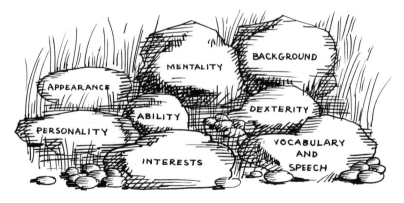

Individual Differences

Appearance	Dexterity
Mentality	Ability
Background	Interests
Personality	Vocabulary and speech

In order to measure individual differences, psychologists have devised various tests. Some are used to classify intelligence. One of these is the IQ or intelligence quotient test. Another test, one used in the military, is the GCT or General Classification Test. Both tests are similar in that the results form a general pattern in which an IQ of 100 is considered average, while an IQ of 85 is considered below average. The scores for most people fall near the average score for the test, with fewer and fewer people in the groups as the scores go much above or below the average.

Among other tests, some have been designed to measure a person's manual skill, his personality structure, his needs, interests, attitudes, and what he might want or expect from life.

The more you know about a person, the more qualified you are to be a good supervisor. So if results of any such tests are available, take time to find out how your workers performed. A word of caution, however: your purpose in examining any information like this is to help you do your job better, and you should not seek such information merely out of curiosity. You will, of course, treat all such information confidentially and not discuss it with fellow workers.

Besides using test results and other information available in personnel folders, you will find it worth while
to keep your eyes and ears open and be alert to whatever other information comes your way about your
workers.

So you say, "All right, anybody knows people all aren't
the same. How does this help me supervise them?"
Let me tell you about the supervisor in charge of material who, because of a new process, needed someone
to pick out and place an assortment of very small parts
in the proper trays. He knew that one of his boys had
quite a reputation for his skill in tying fishing flies.
The supervisor assigned him to the job and he performed above expectations. The answer to the supervisor's problem was simplified because he had taken
the trouble to learn something about each person who
worked for him.

Let's look at another example. John was an Army
officer whom the company employed soon after his
retirement. He has now been with the company six
months. He is fifteen years older than you. Bill is
the same age as John. Bill was hired by the company
twelve years ago and has slowly worked up to the position of leadman in the group. Would you say that
John or Bill is likely to give you more concern?

1. John...................................Page 30
2. Bill ....Page 31

1. I would say John.

You are correct.

John has a different background, has been working in a different situation, and is fairly new to civilian life and to the company. John might even resent Bill because John feels he has more experience in leading people than Bill has. John might aggressively try to take over some of Bill's assignments.

Because you know something about John's background. you are in a position to understand him and head off any friction in your department. You will help him learn how he can advance the group effort, how he can expect to benefit through loyal service, and so forth.

This example stresses the differences between the backgrounds of two people, and how these differences could possibly affect your supervisory efforts.

▶ Now turn to page 32.

You answered 2. Bill.

This is <u>not</u> the most likely answer.

Perhaps you made this choice because you felt Bill would be worried about having to compete with a retired Army officer, or you may have had other reasons. But we doubt that Bill will give you more concern because you know Bill's record with the company. His position as leadman is an indication of his experience and worth. You and Bill should be able to communicate and easily resolve any problem that might arise.

▶ Please return and select the other answer.

You must try to understand those you are supervising, not only in terms of what motivates them and what their backgrounds are, but also in terms of what can be expected of them. This often ties in with intelligence. Repetitive work bores the quick. A job requiring creative thinking could overwhelm others.

Finding the worker whose desires, skills, and knowledge measure up to the task seems like a hard assignment. In practice you cannot hope for perfection, but you can become skilled at keeping the job moving along if you know your workers before you assign the work.

Now it is time to ask a question to be sure we are thinking along the same lines. We have discussed some of the reasons why people work. We have talked about people as individuals with motivations. We know that for many reasons some workers appear to be more capable than others.

Let us suppose that you have three workers. One is highly motivated to work, another has the highest IQ, and the third has the greatest ability to do the job. An emergency has arisen and you must assign one of these three to get the job done quickly. Which would you choose?

1. The worker with the highest IQ . . . . Page 33

2. The worker with the ability. . . . . Page 34

3. The worker with the highest motivation. . . Page 36

Your answer was 1. The worker with the highest IQ.

It's sure tempting to go along with those brains, isn't it? But what good is intelligence if the person hasn't learned to do the job as well as another? True, alongside of others being taught he might stand out, but our problem is to take care of an emergency by selecting the person most capable of doing the job.

▶ Please return and choose a better answer.

You selected 2. The worker with the ability.

You are correct.

In an emergency we would have to go along with the person we knew had the ability to get the job done. Intelligence and willingness do not necessarily outrank know-how.

Supervisors have to weigh many factors pertaining to people. We should know what motivates our workers, how smart they are, and something about their abilities in reference to the job to be done. If we know these things about each man in our crew, whether it is made up of one man or a dozen, we can feel more confident about assigning work.

Let's proceed to another subject. It seems a workday never passes without the supervisor's imparting some knowledge to his workers in the form of training. Training is perhaps one of the supervisor's most important jobs. This being the case, we should spend time finding out how people learn.

There are many reasons to believe that motivation and learning are tied closely together. The desire to learn something is usually coupled with the desire to succeed, to gain recognition, etc. We are not going to review basic motivations here, but remind you that these could be the factors which compel people to learn. Let's discuss a few of the ways by which we learn.

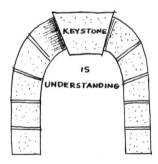

Trial and error is a way of learning by experimenting and discarding approaches that do not yield the desired result. This is like a child's trying to put a square block in a round hole. It doesn't work. So he begins again, trying to find the shape that will match the block.

Practice is learning by repeating over and over again. Here we learn through repetition.

Understanding is the keystone to all learning. If we take the time necessary to explain the whys, the hows, and what is expected of a person, we impart understanding. This is essential to getting maximum performance from him on the job.

Supposing we were put to work on a device which required three operations in sequence before the device would function. We were shown the proper sequence of operations and the results. We performed what we thought was the sequence of operations and nothing happened. We repeated the operation using a different sequence. Which of the learning methods would we be using?

You answered 3. The worker with the highest motivation. Not quite.

Eagerness has its advantages, but not in this case. The person might want to be selected for the task to show you how capable he is, but you can't afford to take this chance in an emergency. We feel there is a better answer to the question.

▶ Please return and try again.

You selected 1. Trial and error.

This is correct.

Repeated below are these learning theories. You might think about how they can be applied on the job.

Trial and error. Even without an instructor it is possible to develop and learn a correct procedure through trying different methods and correcting your errors.

Practice. Constant practice leads to improvement until a satisfactory standard is reached. A good example is learning to play the piano.

Understanding. This is the most important ingredient in the learning process. It involves knowing the meaning, or significance, or what is being learned. It goes beyond just the function or act. When you are training or learning by applying practice or trial and error, try first to gain understanding about the purpose of each step involved and of the way various steps lead to a desired result.

Which one of the following statements is incorrect, according to the definitions given above?

You selected 2. Practice.

No.

We learn from practice by doing a task correctly over and over again. Please review the definitions and reconsider your answer. Pay attention to the short word or words describing the ways we learn and you will have the clue to the right response.

▶ Please return and try again.

You selected 3. Understanding.

This is not correct.

You wouldn't have made this choice if you had carefully noted the cue words describing the various ways we learn. We were not told <u>why</u> the operations were performed in the sequence being taught, nor were we told anything else about the device to give us the "why."

▶ Please return and try again.

1. Repeating an exercise trains one to understand the exercise. You are right in choosing this as the in-correct statement.

A person could learn how to fill out a shipping form without having the faintest idea about how the form is used and the importance of the form to the management. While this knowledge is not vital for the task, knowing why the form is used and its importance as a record and as information for control will make the job more meaningful to the worker.

Before you proceed to the next chapter, "Recognizing Supervising Skills," tackle the following problems so that you can check on how much you have learned about understanding people. This test will serve also as a means of review.

 Here is your first problem.

You were given some of the basic reasons why people work. Only one of the lists below gives two reasons that you should by now have memorized. Select that list.

1. Security	2. Security	3. Security
Leadership	Faith	Companionship
Personality	Trust	Desire to
Ability	Necessity	produce
		Fear
Page 43	Page 44	Page 45

You selected 2. Doing something over and over again is learning by practice.

This statement is correct.

You may be confusing trial and error with practice. Practice means repeating the same thing over and over as accurately as possible until an acceptable standard of skill is reached. You know what you want to accomplish, but lack the necessary skill to do it correctly.

On the other hand, you learn by trial and error when you try various approaches or methods and gradually eliminate mistakes or poor procedures.

▶ Please return and choose the correct answer.

You chose 3. Putting pieces of a jigsaw puzzle together can be accomplished by trial and error.

This is a true statement.

A very complex jigsaw puzzle could be solved this way. Trial and error means to try a solution, and if it proves wrong, to go on trying another until the right solution is reached.

Practice, on the other hand, means repeating the right thing as accurately as possible over and over again in order to gain skill and efficiency.

▶ Please return and select the correct answer.

You selected list 1:

    Security
    Leadership
    Personality
    Ability

No.

Security is one of the basic reasons why people work. None of the other reasons were given in the list we asked you to remember. You should try hard to remember the correct list because your job as a supervisor involves or will involve, more than anything else, an understanding of people. Knowing what motivates people is basic to being able to understand them.

▶ Proceed to page 45. Review the list of basic reasons why people work, then continue to the second review problem.

You selected 2.

    Security
    Faith
    Trust
    Necessity

Uh-uh!

Security is the only word in this list which you were told was a reason why people work. It is important that you understand the reasons which motivate people to work. Knowing these reasons will help you as a supervisor because most of your time will be spent directing people.

▶ Proceed to page 45 and review the list of basic reasons why people work. Then continue to your second review problem.

You chose 3.

    Security
    Companionship
    Desire to produce
    Fear

You are right.

The complete list you were asked to remember is

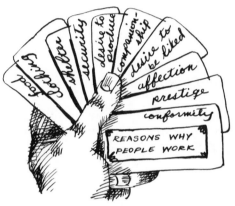

Food
Clothing
Shelter
Security
Desire to
   produce
Companionship
Desire to be
   liked
Affection
Prestige
Conformity

Now for your second review problem. People are different in their looks, levels of intelligence, backgrounds, and (   ).

Supply the missing word from the following choices. It is one we covered in our lesson.

1. Nationality . . . . Page 46

2. Friends . . . . Page 47

3. Ability. . . . . Page 48

4. Political party. . . . . Page 49

(from page 45)

1. Nationality.

This is not the right selection.

A person's nationality might possibly make him look different, behave differently, or have different standards from someone else, but nationality is not the word we asked you to remember about individual differences. Here is the list of important individual differences we gave you:

Appearance	Dexterity
Mentality	Ability
Background	Interests
Personality	Vocabulary and speech

In our question about individual differences, the correct missing word was Ability.

▶ Please proceed to page 48 and review question 3.

2. Friends.

This is not the correct answer.

If the person's friends were artists it wouldn't necessarily make his attitude toward his job different from anyone else's. It would be unreasonable to judge a man by his friends. Here is the complete list of the individual differences given in the lesson:

Appearance	Dexterity
Mentality	Ability
Background	Interests
Personality	Vocabulary and speech

The correct answer to the question was <u>Ability</u>.

▶ Please proceed to page 48 for question 3.

3. Ability.

Very good!

We think you will agree it is useful to know why people differ and that you should learn as much as possible about those who work for you. Particularly, you should know some of the reasons why each person works in your organization and how you can best fit him to the job.

Here is your last review question. We know that the desire to learn springs from some type of motivation. You were told some of the ways people learn. Which of the elements of learning listed below is considered the most essential?

1. Understanding .... Page 50

2. Trial and error .... Page 51

3. Practice or repetition .... Page 52

4. Political party.

No.

Some people might say you were right, but this isn't the correct answer to the question. Go to a large meeting of people and try to determine how the political party they belong to makes them different. Listed below are the individual differences given in the lesson.

Appearance	Dexterity
Mentality	Ability
Background	Interests
Personality	Vocabulary and speech

The missing word was <u>Ability</u>.

▶ Please go back to page 48 for question 3.

1. Understanding.

You are correct.

Understanding is the most essential part of the learning process. This applies to simple as well as complex tasks. We must be sure the worker understands
clearly our instructions as to how he is to do the job,
and that he understands also how his job relates to the
goals of his company.

Let's proceed now to Chapter 3, "Recognizing Supervisory Skills."

▶ Please turn to page 53.

You chose 2. Trial and error.

Whatever gave you that idea?

This is one way people learn, but imagine how much better the task could be done if the learner understood what he was doing and why he was doing it. Even a few instructions can make a job meaningful to the learner.

A brief explanation is better than none. Doing a job without knowing why is not very interesting or stimulating. As a supervisor, part of your job includes helping people get ahead. Letting the worker know why he does a job enriches his knowledge and motivates him in his work. Understanding is essential to real learning.

Now you are ready to proceed to Chapter 3, "Recognizing Supervisory Skills."

▶ Please turn to page 53.

You say 3. Practice or repetition.

Not really.

Practice is one of the ways people learn, but we tried to emphasize understanding as the best way to learn. Practice without meaning is not nearly so effective as practice with a knowledge of why we are practicing.

You will be spending many hours training workers in their jobs. Try to impart understanding and meaning.

Now let's go to Chapter 3, "Recognizing Supervisory Skills."

▶ Please turn to page 53.

Recognizing
Supervisory Skills

A basic rule about supervision is this:

"A supervisor must be effective at getting results through the efforts of other people."

In Chapter 2 we discussed some of the concepts that we should grasp in order to understand people. The next step is to learn how to recognize and apply supervisory skills. First of all, you will agree that you must know the job well yourself. Indeed, you must feel secure in that knowledge. You should be able to recognize talent in others and not be afraid of it.

Good supervisors are not necessarily born to the call-
ing. Some supervisors may demonstrate a high degree
of leadership skills. By doing so they appear to come
by these skills naturally. Some of us may be gifted
with the knack of getting along with people and appear
to be what is often termed "a born leader." There is
no reason why you should feel at a disadvantage if you
place yourself outside the leader category. Skillful
supervision <u>can be learned</u>. It just takes some application on your part.

In order to be effective we must demonstrate certain skills. We are going to list some of these and then ask your opinion as to how these skills pertain to you and your job.

Bringing out the best in people	Making decisions
	Delegating work
Getting things done	Training
Cooperating	Communicating

Chances are you will recognize some of the skills you personally have down pat. Let's say you're really good at getting things done. As for the others, you could improve yourself on some, and maybe there are one or two items on this list which you'd just as soon not have to think about. Our question is this: Is it better to concentrate on and improve in the areas where you are weakest, or is it better to concentrate on improving the skills you already have?

1. Concentrate on improving your
   weak points .... Page 55

2. Keep improving on the skills you have..... Page 58

1. Your answer was that you should concentrate on improving your weak points. Certainly!

The skills you are applying well can wait. Surely you are not suddenly going to forget how to use them. All of us should constantly be improving ourselves, but concentrating hardest in the areas of our jobs where we know we are weak. Please note that we do not imply you should stop improving your strong points. Self-improvement all along the line should be a continuing process.

Now self-analysis asks us to perform an act which is almost alien to many of us. One of the most difficult tasks facing the supervisor is that of analyzing himself. Sometimes it hurts the ego to have to admit one's weaknesses.

To help you determine where you could stand some improvement, we are going to enumerate some supervisory skills and ask you to grade yourself. Use the

numeral (1) for the skill you feel is among your best, (2) for the next best, and so on. Then take the list and have someone who knows you well, perhaps your own supervisor, grade you in the same manner.

You may have a better or worse impression of yourself than others have. The other person may not agree with how you score yourself. By comparing his opinion with yours, you may decide to modify your opinion. You shouldn't be hesitant about doing this because chances are you will be spending some of your supervisory time grading others. This will be good practice.

Above all, you shouldn't let your feelings be hurt by finding that someone else disagrees with what you may have considered one of your strong points. After all, you wouldn't have been placed in a supervisory position if those over you hadn't felt you were competent.

Here is the list of supervisory skills and a few key words of explanation:

Bringing out the best in people (helping, encouraging — not hindering)

Getting things done (organizing, planning, setting and achieving goals)

Cooperating (being willing to work with others, having respect for others both up and down the line)

Making decisions (weighing the facts and acting upon them)

Being self-confident (believing in your ability, having faith in your judgment)

Delegating work (giving others the responsibility and authority to act)

Training (teaching work skills to others)

Communicating (passing along information precisely and clearly)

You probably know it isn't good enough just to agree there are some supervisory skills which you aren't applying as well as you should. You must decide to work at improving these skills. How do you go about this? There is no standard pattern of learning which applies equally well to all individuals. Perhaps some examples will give you a clue.

Let's start with bringing out the best in people. Bringing out the best in people means helping them use their enthusiastic, ambitious, and creative desires on the job. To do this we must treat the workers fairly, encourage them, and create an atmosphere of teamwork.

Supposing you had just assigned someone to keep raw materials always available at a machine. The operator of the machine tells you he has run out of work because the raw material box is empty. What should you do?

1. Find the person responsible for keeping
   the box filled with raw material and
   bawl him out right on the spot .... Page 59

2. Find the man and take him to your
   office where you can bawl him out in
   private .... Page 60

Your answer was 2. Keep improving on the skills you have. This is important <u>but</u>...

You will recall that we said <u>skillful supervision can be learned</u>. The skills you possess probably will stick with you, and you should keep improving on them, BUT it is more important to know which are your weaker skills.

▶ So please return and select the other answer.

You selected 1. Find the person responsible for keeping the box filled with raw material and bawl him out on the spot.

We think this would be a serious mistake.

If you do this, you will embarrass the man and could even embarrass the workers who overhear you. Bawling people out in public leads to low morale. Low morale leads to poor work and inefficiency.

▶ Please return and pick the other answer.

You selected 2. Find the man and take him to your office to bawl him out in private.

While neither action offers a good solution to the problem, this is the better answer. The man may have an excuse for not having the job done. Maybe you will have to tell him to come to you immediately if the supply of materials should become exhausted, for instance. The real point is you must show regard for people's feelings. You must be able to discipline people, even to crack down if necessary, without hurting their feelings. You must be able to point out errors tactfully. Bawling someone out in front of others, or even in private, seldom accomplishes your purpose. Get the facts and if the person responsible has failed, let him know how you want things done and that you expect they will be done right the next time. If part of the fault is yours, don't be afraid to admit it.

Suppose you ask the person you were going to bawl out, "How come you didn't keep the box filled with material like I told you?" and he answers, "I thought you told me to carry the processed parts into the paint shop and I didn't have time to get to the paint shop and back before the box was empty."

Which would you say?

1. "Why don't you listen to what I tell you?"...Page 62

2. "All right. Let's go over it again."....... Page 63

3. "I don't want any excuses. Your job is to keep the raw material box loaded."..... Page 65

1. "Why don't you listen to what I tell you?"

This isn't the best answer.

Maybe the man listened, but your instructions didn't get across. Or maybe he did follow instructions to the letter, and for this very reason the material box was empty before he could finish another task you had assigned to him.

▶ Please return and select a better answer.

2. You would say, "All right. Let's go over it again."
This is the best answer.

Chances are your instructions were either unclear or
incomplete. It is very important for you to be sure
people <u>understand</u> your instructions and that they are
capable of performing the assignment. It's possible,
too, that the work is not being channeled to the best
advantage. Imagine trying to work at a job when you
aren't quite sure what you are supposed to be doing.
You'd worry, wouldn't you, wondering if your supervisor were going to bawl you out for not doing the job
the way he intended it to be done?

Disciplining people only in private and giving clear
instructions are two of the ways we <u>bring out the best</u>
in people. Treating people fairly, and having faith in
them, are other ways of keeping morale at a high level.

Decision making is another supervisory skill that could
be the subject of an entire book. Top executives and
employees on every level are confronted daily with
problems requiring decisions, just as you are. Here
are some guidelines you will find useful.

1. Clearly identify the problem (write it down if
   this will help you).

2. Get the facts.

3. Weigh the facts and evaluate them.

4. Consider the alternatives.

5. Make the decision and act.

6. Follow up, evaluate, revise as necessary.

These six steps in the decision-making process are in an unalterable sequence. Please memorize them in the order listed.

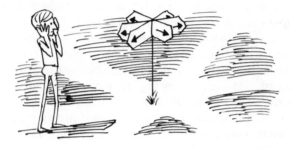

For an example of the process of decision making, let's go back to the person assigned the job of keeping the material box loaded. The machine operator reports he is out of work because the material box is empty. The worker assigned to keep the material box filled says he can't get the processed parts to the paint shop and return in time to refill the material box. You think you understand the problem and decide to use two material boxes so that the machine operator can continue working while the processed parts are being moved to the paint shop. Not long after you have made this decision the machine operator comes to you complaining that he is again out of material. Which step did you fail to consider?

1. Get the facts, weigh the facts, and
   evaluate them ....Page 66

2. Consider alternatives ....Page 67

3. Follow up, evaluate, and revise the
   decision as necessary ....Page 68

3. "I don't want any excuses! Your job is to keep the material box loaded."

If you said this, the man would be completely frustrated. It appears from the worker's reasons that either your instructions were not clear, or you gave him an impossible job assignment. If you expect to command respect and keep production and morale high you must be fair.

▶ Please return and select a better answer.

1. Get the facts, weigh the facts, and evaluate them.
Right you are!

When you learn that one person cannot keep the machine operator supplied with material, you must find
out how long it should take, on the average, to move
the processed parts to the paint shop, and how fast the
machine operator goes through material. With these
additional facts, you can work toward a good decision.

Incidentally, making decisions is closely allied with
getting things done. The ability to organize, plan, and
set and achieve goals requires the ability to make good
decisions. If you haven't done so already, jot down
the guidelines for making decisions.

To continue, let's relax for a minute and discuss
leadership. In most organizations, the leadmen, the
foremen, the supervisors, and the managers are considered leaders. Their jobs have much to do with
directing and showing people how to get things done.
We have listed below three statements which describe
leadership. Which do you think best tells what a leader
should do?

1. Look after and direct..................Page 69

2. Show the way ....Page 70

3. Guide or handle with authority..........Page 72

Your answer was 2. Consider alternatives.

Let's review the problem. The machine operator is out of work because the material box is empty. The person says he can't get to the paint shop with the processed parts and back in time to fill the box before it is completely emptied.

While it is true you probably could find some alternatives to solve the problem, the decision made was improper for another reason.

▶ Please return to page 64 and think about the problem again.

(from page 64)

Your answer was 3. Follow up, evaluate, and revise the decision as necessary. No.

This cannot be the correct answer because you haven't had time to get to this procedure. We said that the decision-making process was very important and that the sequence of steps could not be altered. Which earlier step wasn't followed?

▶ Please return and try to select the right answer.

You selected 1. Look after and direct.

No, not exactly.

This is a definition for supervision. Supervision and leadership are closely allied. The three statements are hard to separate because leadership, management, and supervision are so similar in meaning.

▶ Please turn to page 70.

You selected 2. Show the way.

Good!

To look after and direct is a definition for supervision, and to guide or handle with authority is a definition for management. The definition for leadership is to show the way. Of course, there is a good deal of overlapping in these definitions.

Every supervisor is expected to have leadership qualities. In addition to taking the initiative, an important one of the leadership skills depends on your taking the right approach to the people you supervise. You should avoid being domineering, you should not talk down to people, and you should remember to request rather than command. Workers will respect you more if you can maintain discipline and be firm without throwing your weight around. Morale and company spirit will also be higher.

Consider the following example:

Smith has just been made supervisor of the shipping department. This department has had a poor record for some time. The first thing Smith does is address all the people under his supervision with, "I'm not going to tolerate any mistakes, or any excuses for not being on the job on time, or any laziness. You people have a job to do and I'm here to see that you do it. Anybody who doesn't like it can quit!"

The four leadership skills we have just mentioned are:

(a) Taking the initiative

(b) Not being domineering

    (c) Not talking down to your workers

    (d) Making requests, instead of commanding

In Smith's case, which of these skills did he use to "show the way"?

1. (a) ....Page 73

2. (b), (c), (d) ....Page 75

3. None of these........................Page 76

You selected 3. Guide or handle with authority.

To guide or handle with authority is a definition for management. Did you notice how much alike these phrases were? The reason for presenting all three was to impress upon you that leadership is akin to supervision and management.

▶ Please turn back to page 70.

You chose 1.(a). Taking the initiative.

You are right.

Smith didn't follow any of the other leadership skills, but he did take the initiative. He did call a meeting for the purpose of improving the shipping department's performance.

Let us suppose Smith had called the meeting and said to his workers, "As you all know, I've recently been appointed your supervisor. This department's record hasn't been the greatest, but I think if we all work together, we can make a better showing. Doing a good job makes us all proud of our work and lets the Company know we are capable. I, for one, welcome any suggestions and plan to talk to each and every one of you to get your ideas as to how to do the job better and how we can work as a team. Why not gain recognition from the company that this is their best department? We have to improve. I will take whatever steps necessary so that we can improve and work as a team.

I will be contacting each of you soon. Let's solve these problems together."

This approach goes further toward what we mean by showing the way. Now Smith is going to talk with each individual working for him. In this way he can show interest in them as well as in the job. There's no "hard talk" here to offend anyone. He shows respect while being firm about the problem.

Somewhere along the way you have probably heard someone say, "You've got to hand it to Joe; he used to blow up, but since he became a supervisor he has controlled his temper." Would you say Joe accomplished this because he (   )?

1. Evaluated himself?.....................Page 77

2. Wanted others to like him?..............Page 80

You answered 2. (b), (c), and (d).

No.

You didn't read the question correctly. We asked, "What skills did Smith use to show the way?"

▶ Please return and try to give the right answer.

You selected 3. None of these.

We disagree.

Smith talked to all his people and in effect said, "Produce or get out!" We want you to recognize that Smith did take action. To find the right answer, you must ask yourself how we described this action.

▶ Go back to the question again on page 71. We're sure you will get the correct answer.

You chose 1. He evaluated himself.

You are correct.

You are probably aware that the development of leader-ship traits requires self-evaluation, as does the development of leadership skills. Bringing out the best in people, making good decisions, and communicating properly, for instance, could well depend upon your ability to use self-control. Emotional stability is a very important leadership trait.

In a sense, we could summarize our discussion of leadership, or showing the way, by stating that the proper application of supervisory skills will also bring about true leadership. The two go together. The harder you work at improving your leadership quali-ties, the more you will improve your potential as an effective supervisor. We can demonstrate this point in another way. Below is a list of the basic supervisory skills or abilities we think you should learn to apply. Alongside is a list of leadership traits. You will notice that the two lists seem to go together.

Supervisory abilities	Leadership applications
1. Bringing out the best in people	1. Speaking to people as equals
2. Getting things done	2. Taking the initiative
3. Cooperating	3. Respecting superiors and subordinates
4. Making decisions	4. Showing firmness and determination
5. Delegating work	5. Having no favorites
6. Training	6. Demonstrating an interest in each person
7. Communicating	7. Letting people know in advance things which will affect them

Have you observed that all the abilities we have been discussing relate to your dealing with people? This explains why it is so important to understand what motivates people, how they differ, one from another, and how they learn.

There is another supervisory trait which you should have. A supervisor's job is often full of compromises. We have people working for us who are not up to the tasks. We should try to find jobs more suitable for them, but it isn't always possible. We are supposed to get something done within certain time limits. We don't make it, so we look around for reasons why we didn't perform or we look for excuses. And you must admit, every job has areas where the truth can be shaded just a little. We can stretch the work, we can make the figures look good, or we can pad the expense account.

Just as we demand honesty from our workers, we must demand honesty from ourselves. It isn't always easy. Our pride may get in the way. We simply hate to admit our mistakes sometimes.

Let's look for just a minute at some definitions. Which do you feel best expresses the meaning of the word honest?

1. Not lying, cheating, or stealing .... Page 81

2. Not hiding one's real nature, being
   frank and open...................... Page 82

3. Not mixed with something of less
   value, being genuine .... Page 83

2. He wanted others to like him.

No.

He might have changed before if this were so. We want you to recognize that leadership and supervision go hand-in-glove, so to speak. Earlier we discussed the need for self evaluation in order to find out which supervisory skills you should try to improve. Here Joe has followed a similar course and has improved his leadership skills.

▶ Please return and select the correct answer.

You selected 1.

You feel not lying, cheating, or stealing best expresses the meaning of the word honest.

▶ Please turn to page 84.

You chose 2.

You feel that not hiding one's real nature, being frank and open, best expresses the meaning of the word honest.

▶ Please turn to page 84.

You went along with 3.

You feel that not being mixed with something of less value, being genuine, best expresses the meaning of the word honest.

▶ Please turn to page 84.

You had to select one of the following as best describing honest:

1. Not lying, cheating, or stealing
2. Not hiding one's real nature, being frank and open
3. Not mixed with something of less value, being genuine

Each of these three selections defines one facet of the word honest.

We wanted you to look them over. While the first selection is the most commonly understood meaning, the other two are equally valid. When we put on an act to hide what we are really thinking, or when we water down the facts just a trifle, we are not being honest.

Our study about recognizing supervisory skills has covered quite a bit of ground. The following questions will serve to emphasize those points which we feel are most important for you to remember.

You were asked to study a list of certain supervisory skills. Which of the following was <u>not</u> one of these skills?

1. Getting things done....................Page 85

2. Training ....Page 86

3. Identifying the problem ....Page 87

4. Communicating ....Page 88

Your answer was 1. Getting things done.

Sorry, you are incorrect.

Getting things done was included in the list of supervisory skills. The complete list you were asked to
study was:

>   Bringing out the best in people
>   Making decisions
>   Getting things done
>   Delegating work
>   Training
>   Communicating

Identifying the problem was not in this list. It is,
however, one of the steps we use in coming to a decision.

▶ Please turn to page 87 for your next question.

You selected 2. Training.

No.

Training was included in the list of supervisory skills.
The complete list you were asked to study was:

    Bringing out the best in people
    Cooperating
    Getting things done
    Making decisions
    Delegating work
    Training
    Communicating

Identifying the problem was not in this list. This is
one of the steps we use in coming to a decision.

▶ Please proceed to page 87 for your next question.

You chose 3 as being out of place in this list.

Very good!

    Identifying the problem is one of the steps in <u>making decisions</u>, however. Which of the following is <u>not</u> one of the five additional steps?

1. Get the facts .... Page 89

2. Weigh the facts and evaluate them ...... Page 90

3. Anticipate likely causes .... Page 91

4. Make the decision and act.............. Page 92

5. Follow up, evaluate, revise as
    necessary............................. Page 93

(from page 84)

Your answer was 4. Communicating.

This is not right.

Communicating <u>was</u> included in the list of supervisory skills. The comp<u>lete</u> list you were asked to study was:

Bringing out the best in people
Cooperating
Getting things done
Making decisions
Delegating work
Training
Communicating

<u>Identifying the problem</u> is one of the steps we use in making decisions.

▶ Please turn back to page 87 for your next question.

You chose 1. Get the facts.

No, this is not the answer.

After identifying the problem, the next steps in the decision-making process are:

> Weigh the facts and evaluate them.
> Consider the alternatives.
> Make the decision and act.
> Follow up, evaluate, revise as necessary.

The statement that does not belong in the list we gave you is <u>Anticipate likely causes</u>.

▶ Please turn to page 91.

2. Weigh the facts and evaluate them.

No.

This is one of the steps in the decision-making process. The incorrect step is "anticipate likely causes." The proper step after weighing and evaluating the facts is to Find out what alternatives there are.

Here is the list of decision making steps again.

1. Identify the problem.
2. Get the facts.
3. Weigh the facts and evaluate them.
4. Consider the alternatives.
5. Make the decision and act.
6. Follow up, evaluate, revise as necessary.

▶ Please go to page 91.

You have selected 3. Anticipate likely causes, as not one of the steps in making decisions.

You are correct.

In its place should be <u>Consider the alternatives</u>.

Here is your final question. Listed below are three definitions. One best describes management, one best describes supervision, and one best describes leadership. Which of them most clearly defines leadership?

1. Guiding or handling with authority........Page 94

2. Looking after and directing.............Page 95

3. Showing the way......................Page 96

4. Make the decision and act.

No.

The decision-making steps you were asked to remember were:

1. Clearly identify the problem.
2. Get the facts.
3. Weigh the facts and evaluate them.
4. Consider the alternatives.
5. Make the decision and act.
6. Follow up, evaluate, revise as necessary.

Anticipating likely causes is not in this list and should have been your choice of an incorrect answer.

▶ Please turn back to page 91.

5. Follow up, evaluate, revise as necessary.

Your answer is incorrect.

You probably did not read the question properly. We asked you to select the step which was <u>not</u> part of the decision-making process. We expect you knew that <u>Anticipate likely causes</u> was not one of these steps.

Here again are the steps in decision making.

1. Identify the problem.
2. Get the facts.
3. Weigh the facts and evaluate them.
4. Consider the alternatives.
5. Make the decision and act.
6. Follow up, evaluate, revise as necessary.

▶ Please turn back to page 91.

Your choice was 1. Guiding or handling with authority.
No.

This is a better definition for management. Leadership is closely allied to both management and supervision. You may recall we gave three definitions and the one for leadership was <u>showing the way</u>.

▶ Please turn to page 97.

You chose 2. Looking after and directing.

Not quite.

This is the definition we gave you for supervision. You may recall, we gave three definitions — one for management, one for supervision, and one for leadership. We were hopeful you would see that leadership was closely allied with both management and supervision. The definition for leadership is showing the way. There are many traits a supervisor must have, and many skills he must employ in order to show the way.

▶ Please turn to page 97.

3. Showing the way.

You are correct.

You have demonstrated that you recognize some of the skills important to good supervision. This chapter has also given us a little practice in applying some of these skills. Please proceed to Chapter 4, "Supervising People," on page 97.

Supervising People

In this chapter we will discuss some ways in which you can get to know the people who work for you. We will talk about delegating work, communicating, and judging performance. If you apply yourself, you can acquire the ability to work well with people.

In January of 1943, the War Manpower Commission Bureau of Training issued a "Training Within Industry" bulletin, No. 4-D. The subject of this bulletin was "How to Improve Job Relations." It emphasized four basic principles for maintaining good relations with those who work for you.

Here are the four principles:

1. Let each worker know how he is getting along.

2. Give credit where credit is due.

3. Tell people in advance about changes which will affect them.

4. Make the best use of each person's ability.

Taking these principles one at a time, let's discuss keeping each worker posted on how he is getting along.

Assume you have assigned someone a new job. As a good supervisor, you should have talked to this person about how the job fits into the overall scheme of things, discussed the specific job, and made sure the person knew what was expected of him. After a few days have gone by, you observe the worker is not measuring up to the standards established for the job. You decide because the work is new, you will wait to see how the person gets along. After a month at the new job, the worker hasn't improved to your satisfaction. You tell the person, "You're going to have to work harder."

Would you say you were properly applying the principle of letting the worker know how he was getting along?

1. Yes .... Page 99

2. No .... Page 100

Your answer was Yes.

This is incorrect.

You must tell the worker he is not measuring up to the standards for the job as soon as it comes to your attention. Determine why the job is not being done as desired and try to take corrective action. If you wait too long, the worker will ask, "Why didn't you say so sooner?" In the meantime, of course, production is not going on as well as it should be.

▶ Please return and select the right answer.

Your answer was No.

You are correct.

It is important to tell people when they do not measure up to the standards of the job as soon as it comes to your attention. Chances are there are reasons for the poor performance and the sooner these are brought to light, the sooner the job standard will be met. Letting people know how they stand through earned praise or by just criticism gives them a chance to feel they are important to you and to the job.

The next principle is giving credit where credit is due. Each worker, or section, or department deserves to know when a good job is done. If someone gives you credit which was earned by a team effort, pass the credit along to the whole team. It will be appreciated.

Let's take a typical application of this principle. You have five workers we will call A, B, C, D, and E. For some time the company has been using a rating system in evaluating its employees. You personally

like A as an individual over the other four workers.
Worker A doesn't watch the clock and leave as soon
as the whistle blows. He applies himself and is constantly taking training courses for self-improvement.
While B, C, D, and E are all good workers, they do
not quite measure up to A in capability. You reflect
this in your rating of these five workers. Your assist-
ant is transferred to another department and you decide to offer A this job. Select one of the following
answers as your appraisal of this decision.

1. This is a case of favoritism............Page 102

2. This gives credit where credit is due ....Page 103

You selected 1. This is a case of favoritism.

Why?

The worker in question is not to blame because the supervisor likes him. If you want to, you can classify this as a side advantage. Actually, we would like all our workers to improve themselves. We would like them all to be so interested in their work that time doesn't register with them as the day comes to a close.

▶ Please return and select the right answer.

Your answer was 2. This gives credit where credit is due.

You are correct.

If it weren't for the company's rating system, you might unwittingly be accused of showing favoritism for A whom you liked best of all the five workers. Encouraging a person who deserves to get ahead is not favoritism at all. It is an application of the principle of giving credit where credit is due.

Our third principle is telling people in advance about changes that will affect them. An action as simple as a little change in your routine can cause major disturbances in people. Did you ever have the feeling your supervisor was mad at you? For some unknown reason he hadn't spoken to you for a couple of days, let's say. Normally he made it a point to say at least a word or two every day. A little thing, perhaps, but quite significant. Maybe he figured you could get along without that daily word, but he failed to tell you this.

While we can't always tell people in advance the things
which may affect them, we should try hard to do so
when it is possible. The worker should be protected
against being taken by surprise.

The fourth principle of good relations with workers is
making the best use of each person's ability. Repetitive work can be boring to a person who enjoys challen-
ges, while creative thinking could overwhelm another.
People differ in their speed of action, in their willingness to assume the initiative, and in how they adjust
to the job. While you are not expected to be a psy-
chologist, you should try to fit the person to the job.
Don't be afraid to give each person as much and as
responsible work as he can handle.

Before we continue, we want to test your understanding
of these four principles for maintaining good relations
between you and those who work with you. Consider
the following, which is a case study from a Forest Service Basic Supervision Training Manual:

> Jim Jones, a new employee of the Forest Ser-
> vice, had been hired as a foreman. He was
> assigned to take over a crew that had been work-
> ing without a foreman for about six weeks. The
> crew didn't like this new arrangement.

> Soon the District Ranger came out to check with
> Jim. He told Jim that he noticed a let-up in the
> production of the crew since Jim's employment.
> Jim told the Ranger that the crew didn't like
> having a boss with them all the time. He, Jim,
> had also noticed the difference in production
> after checking some old records. Jim and the

Ranger talked it over and the Ranger said, "All right, I'll check with you the latter part of next week."

So Jim started the new week off with a little friendly competition between each of the men and himself. As the week progressed, production steadily increased. By Friday it had nearly doubled. When the Ranger returned, he was so satisfied that he gave a complimentary talk to the whole crew.

With just a few reminders to the crew of their Ranger's recognition of the crew's success, the production stayed at peak the remaining ten weeks that the group was together.

The four basic principles for good relations with your workers are:

  (a) Let each worker know how he is getting along.

  (b) Give credit where credit is due.

  (c) Tell people in advance about changes which will affect them.

  (d) Make the best use of each person's ability.

In the case history above, the Ranger violated one of these principles and applied two of them. Which of the statements below best describes this?

1. Principle (a) is violated and principles (b) and (c) apply.................Page 107

2. Principle (b) is violated and principles (c) and (d) apply.................Page 108

3. Principle (c) is violated and principles (a) and (b) apply.................Page 109

You say: Principle (a) is violated and principles (b) and (c) apply.

Not quite.

During his first visit, the Ranger did not let each worker know how he was getting along. This is true. But you must admit this was Jim Jones' direct responsibility, not the Ranger's. The Ranger did let Jones know how he was getting along and later praised all the men. Therefore, principle (a), let each worker know how he is getting along, was not violated.

▶ Please return and select a better answer.

You say: Principle (b) is violated and principles (c) and (d) apply.

The Ranger did give credit where credit was due. But the Ranger apparently hadn't told the crew about the new foreman. So this doesn't seem to be a good answer.

▶ Please return and try to select the right answer to the question.

Your answer is 3. Principle (c) is violated and principles (a) and (b) apply.

Very good.

The fact the men didn't like having a new boss would indicate they weren't told in advance about this arrangement. Being unprepared, they did not cooperate. The Ranger told Jim Jones how he was getting along and when the work improved, gave credit where it was due. There is the possibility, of course, that the Ranger suggested to Jim that he work with the men and set an example instead of bossing them around.

This Forest Service Case Study also shows us you cannot delegate work without some preliminary planning. The people involved must be considered along with the job to be performed. Before delegating a job, the supervisor must know the job thoroughly and be able to break the job down to its basic elements, obtain the required facts about each step, then determine how and in what sequence the job is to be performed. Occasionally, setting an example by doing the job yourself as Jim did will command the respect of subordinates

and encourage them. With preliminary knowledge, the people can be fitted to the job.

Another element of the job delegation is training. The very fact a person works for you will necessitate your doing a certain amount of training. You probably have experienced by now the TELL, SHOW, ILLUSTRATE steps used for training purposes.

You may have heard of the expression "Learning Curve." When people are taught something new, they tend to learn more rapidly in the beginning, to slow down as time goes on. This can be shown graphically by a curve which rises significantly at first and then tends to level off. Which of the following indicates best what this type of job learning curve shows us?

1. Some people learn more than others .... Page 111

2. The learner can be expected to slow
   down his learning pace somewhere
   along the learning process .... Page 112

3. The curve shows individual differences .. Page 114

Your answer is 1. Some people learn more than others.

No. You have selected a wrong answer.

We explained our learning curve tends to level off, or reach a plateau, after its initial rise. This is a graphic representation of the fact that people learn quite rapidly at first and then, after the first grasp of the new material wears off, they learn more slowly. So the learning curve does not show how much is learned; it shows the relative speeds at which subject material is absorbed by a person.

▶ Please return and select a better answer.

You selected 2. The learner can be expected to slow down his learning pace somewhere along the line.

You are correct.

Some people do learn more than others. The prime purpose of a learning curve is not to measure how much is learned. Actually it is an indication of the rate of learning. Experienced training people have recognized and dealt with the problem of the slow-down in learning by trying to inject some extra motivating factors into the training curriculum. For instance, the TELL portion of training might be by motion picture or closed TV. An outside expert in the subject matter might be brought in to break up the daily routine. Remember, training can sometimes be accelerated by motivating devices.

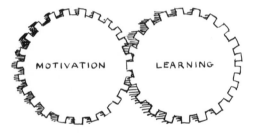

Did you note in our question about learning curves we mentioned that some people learn faster than others? This is another of the individual differences you must take into account in planning an effective training program.

For instance, you may have twelve electricians in your group. Most of the crew are just out of school, but two of the men have worked for the company twenty years. The company decides to switch over from electrical instrumentation to electronic instrumentation. You arrange to have all the crew go to classes to learn how to maintain the new equipment. One of the "old timers" and several of the younger crew members are lagging badly in their class work. Would you say —

1. Apparently they can't learn ?...........Page 115

2. Their learning rate is slower ?.........Page 116

You selected 3. The curve shows individual differences.

No.

The only way you could have selected this answer was if you had assumed that the individual's learning curve could be compared directly with a master curve based on some average of performance. Otherwise you could not judge how well or how poorly he did. Regardless of the learner's ability, job learning curves as a rule show a flattening out after the initial learning period. This is because the worker being trained has a tendency to make rapid progress at the start, and then to progress more slowly.

▶ Please return and select a better answer.

You answered 1. Apparently they can't learn.

You're not getting the message!

People are different. They learn at different speeds. Some take longer to learn than others.

Sometimes people do not read well. They take much longer to finish a page or a chapter of a book than do others. Others may not be able to memorize easily, and have to take longer mastering new material. This doesn't mean they won't learn just as much.

▶ Please return and choose the other answer.

You answered 2. Their learning rate is slower.

This is correct.

Tests have proven that no two people learn at the same speed. But tests also tell us that people who learn slowly, given the same material to learn and allowed to study the material at their own speed, learn just as much as folks who learn more quickly.

Another very basic rule is that you must make sure you are understood. This involves good communication.

To communicate means to pass along.

We communicate information to each other in many ways, by telephone, billboards, blueprints, even with laughter and tears. An organization has many ways of communicating with its workers. We are all familiar with memos, bulletin boards, notices, and meetings. Let's work with some ideas about communicating.

Suppose a meeting has been planned for next Friday. On Wednesday, plans are changed and you are asked to postpone the meeting for a week. How would you communicate this news?

You selected 1. Make every effort, even at extra expense and at some sacrifice of your own time, to let everyone involved know of the change in plans immediately.

Certainly!

One of the basic principles of good relations which applies to communicating is: <u>Let people know in advance things which will affect them.</u>

If you do this you will eliminate one of the reasons for frustration, confusion, and low morale among the workers. Nobody likes to have plans made, only to see them changed at the last minute. Besides, a lot of time is wasted if people are not informed soon enough so that they can reschedule their activities. If this does happen, people tend to grouse and feel that whoever is running things doesn't know what he's doing.

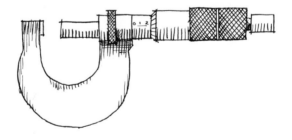

Let's consider another aspect of communication. Let us say that the word "tolerance" means the allowable variation for a given measurement. The tolerance for a measurement is usually expressed as a "plus" or "minus" number. An example would be parts that were four feet long with an allowable tolerance of plus or minus one-eighth of an inch (± 1/8"). In other words, any part four feet long, plus or minus one-eighth of an inch would be acceptable.

Of the choices below, which would you consider to be a close tolerance?

You say: Wait until the original meeting, then tell everyone there of the change in plans. In this way you can save the time and effort required to contact each one individually.

No.

This is not the answer we were hoping for. Time and again, problems arise because people are not informed in advance of events. Just for a minute, imagine what business could have been taken care of if this meeting, which wasn't going to take place, never convened. You owe it to your company and to your fellow workers to value time as money. We do not feel the solution is for you to save your own time at the expense of other people's time.

▶ Please return and select a better answer.

You selected 3. Send a memo to those involved.

No, this can't be the best answer.

While this solution is better than waiting until all are gathered, thus wasting everybody's time, we feel it is more efficient to advise all concerned at the earliest possible moment of the change in plans. In this way, everyone involved can reschedule his time. A memo takes time to circulate, time in which other workers could be rescheduling their activities. You owe it to your company and to your fellow workers to value time as money.

▶ Please return and select the proper answer.

You chose 1. Plus or minus one-half mile.

Of course this isn't the right answer.

We suppose you chose it because it seemed so ridiculous you wanted to find out what we would say.

The fact is, if you were talking about the tolerance of a shot to a spot on the moon, plus or minus one-half mile would be a very close tolerance. To determine how close a tolerance is for a given measurement, we have to know what is being measured.

▶ Please return and choose a better answer.

You chose 2. Plus or minus one-half inch.

Well, maybe.

If you were measuring the distance from here to the moon this would be an extremely close tolerance. But what if you were making a storm door which had to fit a specific area? Measurements with a tolerance of plus or minus one-half inch would hardly satisfy. To determine how close a tolerance is required, we have to know what is being measured.

▶ Please return and select a better answer.

3. Plus or minus one one-thousandth of an inch.

Perhaps.

For most measurements this would be a close toler-ance. But what if you were measuring the width of a molecule? To determine how close a tolerance is re-quired for any given measurement, we must know what is being measured.

▶ Please return and select a better answer.

You chose 4. All the above.

You are correct.

You recognized that the closeness of a tolerance would depend upon what was being measured and that our question failed to make this clear. Plus or minus one-half mile would be a very close tolerance if you were measuring the distance to Mars. Try to make sure your instructions or communications are not misleading. The worker should not have to explain a poor or badly performed job by saying, "Why, I thought you meant..."

Be sure people understand what you are saying!

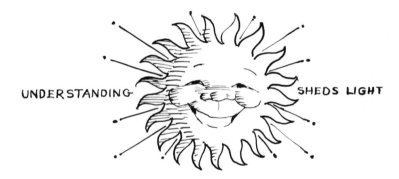

UNDERSTANDING   SHEDS LIGHT

The same words have different meanings for different people, depending upon such things as their education, background, etc. You can waste a lot of time trying to give instructions to someone when your directions mean a certain thing to you but something quite different to the person you are instructing.

Some jobs seem to create the need for a language of their own, particularly jobs which are highly specialized or ones in certain specific industries. Have you ever attended a meeting or conference where the speaker used words unfamiliar to you? This special "talk" using technical words and expressions is often referred to as jargon. When we use jargon in our communications, we get the message across only to those who understand this special language. Special words have a way of becoming second nature to us, particularly when their use is part of our daily routine. We take them for granted, but we must try to bear in mind the fact that new workers or outsiders may not understand us.

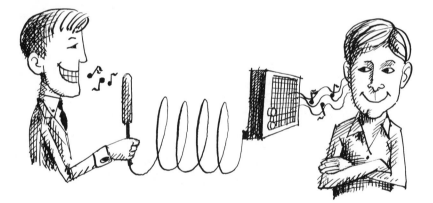

A typical example of jargon would be the case where a system is used as a method for doing something. The code for this system is 222. A small group uses the system. One of the members of the small group goes to a large meeting and gives a speech. He says during the speech, "We use the 222 system and feel it is the most advanced technique known." Nobody knows what he's talking about.

The same could be said about many things we know, particularly those things with which we are very familiar. Sometimes to make sure we are being understood, we should ask questions or ask the other person to repeat to us what we have just told him. We must be sure the sender and receiver are on the same wavelength.

Which would you say is the better way to make yourself understood?

1. Discuss the subject in small steps ...... Page 128

2. Occasionally get some feedback
   during the discussion.................. Page 129

You chose 1. Discuss the subject in small steps.

This isn't the right answer.

Even though you discuss the subject one small step at a time, you may use terms or expressions which the listener does not comprehend. Perhaps your instructions are confusing to him. Breaking the discussion down into small steps may be helpful, but the old technique of asking questions or requesting a demonstration at some strategic point is the better way because it shows you whether or not you are being understood.

▶ No, please return and select the other answer.

You chose 2. Get some feedback.

We agree with you.

The only way you can be sure that you are being understood is by occasionally getting some feedback during
the discussion. From time to time we must ask questions or ask the other person to explain it to us. Here
is another question.

Which do you think is more common, communication
by writing or by talking?

1. Communicating by writing .... Page 130

2. Communication by talking............. Page 131

Your answer is 1. The most common form of communication is by writing.

No.

If everything spoken during any one day were put in writing, we would all be up to our necks in paper. Talking is so common its importance as a means of communication can be easily overlooked.

▶ Please return and select a better answer.

You voted for 2. The most common form of communication is talking.

You are right.

Talking back and forth between people is a fairly continuous process and in usage and importance far outweighs any other form of communication.

To help you develop your skill in communication, let us consider a few established concepts which have to do with talking.

1. We learn about what is going on around us by observing and by listening to others. It is of utmost importance for the supervisor to be a good patient listener.

2. What a speaker says doesn't always convey what he has in mind.

3. Because people's backgrounds vary, things said to one person may have a different meaning for him than they have for the speaker or for others.

4. People tend to resist change itself, and particularly ideas which would change something they have learned to believe. They may even, consciously or unconsciously, warp the idea to fit what they want to believe.

Concepts 2 and 3 are really two sides of the same coin. In other words, two variables are present in any communication. In the first place, you must realize that your ideas and even the words you use depend on your own background. But what the words and ideas mean

to the person who hears them depends on his individual
background which may be quite different. Each of us
interprets and relates new information to a frame-
work of personal knowledge and ideas.

While all these concepts of communication are important, which one is considered outstanding?

Your answer was 1. Listening.

You are correct.

It seems to be human nature to want to be listened to instead of having to listen. How many times have you been interrupted while talking? How many significant thoughts or ideas are missed because we don't practice the art of listening? Just as it takes two to tango, it takes two to communicate — the talker and the listener. It is most important to remember that you are communicating by listening.

We would like to discuss one other form of communication which is important to both the worker and the supervisor. Quite often we communicate to the worker as to how he is doing on his job by means of rating his work against a standard. The standard established for a given piece of work should be a fair one, and the worker should understand it.

Performance standards serve several other purposes. They tell the worker what is expected of him, and they tell the supervisor when a worker requires additional training or is misplaced in the job because of a lack of the necessary abilities.

Would you say performance standards can demoralize the worker?

1. Yes .... Page 138

2. No .... Page 139

You say 2. Making sure what the speaker says is what
he has in mind. We think there is a more important
concept.

While this is an important factor, and one you will find
occasion to deal with, there is a concept of communication which is not specific to just some occasions. It
applies to all oral communication.

▶ Please return and select a better answer.

You chose 3. Making sure the meaning is the same for everyone.

We feel there is a better answer.

You will have to use this concept from time to time, particularly when you have some reason to feel the meaning of the conversation is not clear to everyone. You must decide the answer to our question by finding that concept which is true of all conversations, regardless of subject.

▶ Please return and try to select a better answer.

Your selection was 4. Overcoming resistance to an idea which alters previous beliefs.

This is not the answer we were looking for.

Every now and then an occasion will arise where you will be required to change or introduce something new, and this change will create resistance, the "it isn't the way we used to do it" type of thing. We want you to look for the concept which is true of all oral communications.

▶ Return and see whether you can select the right answer.

Your answer was 1. Yes, performance standards can demoralize the worker. In some cases this is true.

A NO answer would have been just as good here. Performance standards are a management tool. When properly used, they serve many purposes. Some of these are listed below.

Long-range savings
High worker morale
Highlighting training needs
Upgrading workers

Whether or not the employee is demoralized depends upon whether or not his performance is approximately close to the accepted average for his job. If he is assigned to a job beneath his capabilities, the standard is meaningless to him. If the job is far beyond his capacity, he may well be discouraged and demoralized.

▶ Please turn to page 140.

Your answer was 2. No, performance standards cannot demoralize the worker.

This is an acceptable answer providing performance standards are fair and properly used.

Strictly speaking, performance standards serve many purposes as a management tool. Some of these are:

Long-range savings
Higher worker morale
Highlighting training needs
Upgrading workers

Whether or not the worker is demoralized by performance standards will depend upon whether or not his performance is fairly close to the standard set for the job. If it is not, the reason why his performance is well above or below the norm should be considered. The job may be beneath his capabilities or it may be that for one reason or another he is unable to meet a regular quota.

▶ Please turn to page 140.

We said earlier the supervision of people entails showing the way, the <u>right</u> way. The right way, of course,
is the safe way. A supervisor should feel a responsibility for the well-being of his workers. The extent
of his responsibility will differ from circumstance to
circumstance, but the safety of his workers must always be kept in mind.

Here is a concrete example. You and your group of
fifty people are assigned to some temporary quarters
because the company has a space problem. The space
is cramped. In fact, telephone lines and electric outlets are rigged along the floor in such a way people
easily stumble over the outlets and lines. The outlets
weren't built for such abuse and begin to wobble and
become loose.

Which should you do?

1. Let each man figure out how to avoid
   the outlets .... Page 141

2. Complain to your superior .... Page 142

3. Call the maintenance department and
   arrange for complete protection for
   every man .... Page 143

1. Let each man figure out how to avoid the outlet.

Not at all!

This is the easy way of course. It is a simple matter to ignore a safety problem — just pretend it doesn't exist. If the day comes when the outlet finally gives way and someone gets hurt, you can blame it on his carelessness. Or can you?

▶ Please return and choose a better answer.

2. Complain to your superior.

We cannot say that this answer is wrong.

We do feel, however, that it isn't the best answer. While you're complaining to your superior, or await- ing some action, a serious accident could occur. No- body is ever blamed for taking the initiative where personnel safety is involved.

▶ Please return and select the correct answer.

3. Call the maintenance department and arrange for complete protection for every man.

You are correct!

This is one time you can be tough. The safety of your employees — the fellows working for you — are your responsibility. You must keep this constantly in mind. There is no excuse for someone's being hurt by an electric shock, for instance, because you didn't report the danger and insist upon corrective action.

Any time you notice a hazard which could affect the safety of any employee, you should report it. Let's take a common occurrence.

You supervise an area which involves workers at various heights constructing test fixtures and conducting tests. It is a "hard hat" area. During a coffee break, a man from the office conducts a group into the area for a tour. Because of the coffee break, he decides not to bother issuing hard hats to the people he is showing around.

Should you —

1. Keep him out of the area until the
   break is over?....................... Page 144

2. Insist he and his group have hard hats
   before entering the area?............. Page 145

3. Tell him when the coffee break will be
   over so he'll be sure to have gone by
   then?................................ Page 146

1. Keep him out of the area until the break is over.

This is not the right move.

Nobody should be allowed in the area without the proper protection. You are responsible for the safety of the people working for you, of course, as well as for the safety of the people coming into the area, but is it necessary to inconvenience the visitors?

▶ Please return and choose a better answer.

2. Insist he and his group have hard hats before entering the area.

You are responsible in this area. Why take a chance?
Make sure everyone is protected at all times. You
must constantly be on the lookout for job hazards and
the observance of safe practices. Protective goggles,
hard hats, and gloves are often a nuisance. Some
safety procedures take a little more time. On the
other hand, life is more fun for a fellow with two hands
instead of one, with two good eyes instead of none.
Keep this in mind.

▶ Please turn to page 147.

146 (from page 143)

You answered 3. Tell him when the coffee break will be over so he'll be sure to be gone by then.

No, this is not the best way to handle the situation.

You cannot be sure all the group will leave the area even though you do tell the office man when work will start again. Nor can you guarantee that something won't fall in the area, even when the men are not working. The safety of the group can be insured only if they all wear hard hats.

Never take chances where safety is concerned.

▶ Please return and select the right answer.

Now you are ready to take a brief quiz to check on how well you understand and remember our discussion about <u>Supervising People</u>.

Here again are the four principles for maintaining good job relations.

(a) Let each worker know how he is getting along.

(b) Give credit where credit is due.

(c) Tell people in advance about changes that affect them.

(d) Make the best use of each person's ability.

Which combination of these principles do you think best demonstrates communicating?

1. (a), (b), and (c)........................Page 148

2. (a) and (c)............................Page 149

3. All of them............................Page 150

1. You selected

   (a) Let each worker know how he is getting along.
   (b) Give credit where credit is due.
   (c) Tell people in advance about changes that affect
       them.

Why not (d) Make best use of each person's ability?

Remember to communicate means to pass along. We
communicate by our actions and decisions. If a person isn't being used in a job which makes the best use
of his ability, he may believe we don't care much
about him, or we haven't thought enough about him to
recognize his true capabilities. In a sense, we are
communicating that he isn't important.

All four basic principles of good job relations demonstrate communicating.

▶ Please proceed to page 150 for your next question.

2. You chose

>   (a) Let each worker know how he is getting along.
>   (c) Tell people in advance about changes that affect
>   them.

We are sorry you made this selection because it indicates you have missed the main idea we wanted you to get about communicating — to pass along.

We communicate to others through our words, actions, and deeds. Let's look again at the job relations principles you decided did not come under the heading of communication.

>   (b) Give credit where credit is due.

>   (d) Make the best use of each person's ability.

Surely both of these require action on your part even if the action is doing nothing. Doing nothing is a form of communicating. For example, doing nothing by not passing credit along or by keeping the worker on an inferior job, might communicate to the worker that you think he is not important.

All four basic principles of good job relations demonstrate communicating.

▶ Please proceed to page 150 for your next question.

You answered 3. All of them.

> (a) Let each worker know how he is getting along.
> (b) Give credit where credit is due.
> (c) Tell people in advance about changes that affect them.
> (d) Make the best use of each person's ability.

You are correct.

You could have decided that (d), making the best use of each person's ability, was not a form of communication. However, remembering our definition for communicating — passing along — we agree that acting on (d) demonstrates an interest in each person.

▶ Our second review question is about learning curves. The learning curve we described showed:

1. Learning curves have to do with the amount of learning.

No, this is the wrong answer.

We discussed learning curves so you would understand that most people are inclined to learn a task at a rapid pace in the early stages of their training. As the learning gets harder, or the initial motivation for being trained wears off, learning tends to slow down. Knowing this, you can examine your training methods to make certain you have provided motivating materials where necessary to maintain a high level of interest.

Our example of a learning curve had to do with the speed or rate of learning a specific task.

▶ Please proceed to page 152 for your next question.

Your answer is 2. The rate of learning.

This is correct.

The rates of learning for Task A, Task B, or Task C have something in common: The initial speed of learning the tasks is more rapid, then tends to level off. The alert supervisor will try to find motivational methods and materials to make the training interesting and stimulating, and thus maintain a satisfactory rate of learning.

Of course we hope you remember that people differ one from another in their individual learning capabilities. The supervisor who recognizes this will make allowances for individual time differences in learning.

▶ Our next question deals with communicating. Which of the following is the best definition for communicating?

1. Talking .... Page 154

2. To pass along .... Page 155

3. Writing .... Page 156

3. Learning curves have to do with the way of learning.

This is wrong.

Learning curves do not reflect the way people learn. We talked about learning curves because we wanted you to recognize that people typically slow down in their rate of learning as the learning gets harder or the initial motivation for learning the new task wears off. If you understand that this is usually true, you won't become discouraged with the people being trained. You will try to find motivational methods and materials to make the training interesting and desirable, and thereby keep up the speed of learning.

▶ Please turn back to page 152 for your next question.

You selected 1. Talking is the best definition for communication.

No.

Talking is the most common form of communicating, but only one of the many ways we communicate.

The definition for communication we wanted you to remember is — to pass along.

▶ Please proceed to page 157 for a summary of what you have been studying.

The best definition for communication is — to pass along.

Very good.

We think this definition is very appropriate and hope you will remember it for a long, long time. In some respects, this could almost be the definition for the main, or chief, responsibility of a supervisor, to pass along or to communicate!

▶ Please turn to page 157 for a summary of what you have been studying.

The best definition for communicating is — writing.

No.

Writing is only one means of communicating. Do you remember the question asking which was the more common form of communicating — talking or writing? Both are forms of communicating, just as frowns and smiles are forms of communicating. To communicate means — to pass along. Try to remember this.

▶ Please proceed to page 157 for a summary of what you have been studying.

CHAPTER 5

Summary

The following comments will be presented as straightforward text. You won't be asked any questions nor will you be required to jump around through the book any more.

Now that you have reached this chapter, we wonder whether you have any idea of the number of concepts which have been discussed. This little book contains a host of thoughts about the basic supervision of people. In this summary, we will review these thoughts as they were presented to you. We want you to study them once more. In this way, you can be sure more of these concepts will "stick" for a long time.

Our first discussion was about your <u>Understanding People</u>. Here are some of the basic reasons people work:

Food	Desire to produce	Affection
Clothing	Companionship	Prestige
Shelter	Desire to be liked	Conformity
Security		

We stressed the importance of <u>knowing</u> your fellow workers. You can find out a great deal about the people you supervise by reviewing their personnel folders, by listening to them, and by observing their actions during various situations — at lunchtime, or during a cigarette break. Two things you must remember — do not seek learning about the people you supervise out of mere curiosity, and do not fail to keep the information confidential. When you read the personnel folder, try to discover from this information the basic reasons why the worker applied for the job. What motivated him? What keeps on motivating him?

Don't be guilty of letting looks deceive you. <u>Don't take people for granted.</u> If you are going to supervise people, you are going to have to find out, sooner or later, how people differ. But what do you know about the people who work for you after you eliminate the obvious differences? Here is the list of individual differences:

Appearances	Dexterity	Mentality
Ability	Background	Interests
Personality	Vocabulary and	
	speech	

You know how your worker looks, and all about his vocabulary and speech. How about the other differences? They may not be so obvious.

There will be times when the worker with the greater skill should be assigned a job, even when someone else is smarter, or more motivated. You, as a supervisor, must measure capabilities against required performance. If you do this, the decision as to whom to assign a certain task will become a great deal easier.

We mentioned training. Do you realize how much of your time is spent, directly or indirectly, in training each of the men you supervise? Almost every time you are confronted by a worker, whether to answer a question, give an explanation, report the results of a conference, or merely describe a demonstration you witnessed, you are training. As our technology becomes more complex, the function of training becomes more important. It is well, then, to understand how people learn. Do you remember the list we gave you for ways by which people learn? Here it is.

Understanding — the reasons WHY
Practice — repetition
Trial and error — if you don't succeed, try it
    a different way

Do you remember where it was explained to you that any form of learning is more effective when an explanation of how to do the task includes also an explanation as to WHY it is performed in that way? How often people light up with understanding, and they say, "Oh, now we see!

We feel you should do several things to improve your abilities as a supervisor. First, you should be able to recognize the skills a supervisor must have. Secondly, you should make an effort to determine where you can

improve upon your own supervisory skills. Here, then, is the list of supervisory skills.

Getting things done   Training
Making decisions   Communicating
Delegating work   Cooperating
Bringing out the best   Being self-confident
    in people

We have been emphasizing that the best way for a person to learn is through <u>understanding</u>. Only by making an honest appraisal of yourself can you understand how best to improve your supervisory skills. So (1) don't fail to make a self-analysis, and then (2) do something about it. Really, there's no point

in having good intentions about self-improvement without any follow-through. Make up your mind where you can improve your capabilities, set some sort of goals or achievement standards, and try to work toward their fulfillment. This can be a very private matter between you and yourself. Recognize that it can be done — and to your advantage!

You should commit to memory the six important steps necessary to make a good decision. These are the decision-making guidelines you were given.

(1) Identify the problem.
(2) Get the facts.
(3) Weigh the facts and evaluate them.
(4) Consider the alternatives.
(5) Make the decision and act.
(6) Follow up, evaluate, revise as necessary.

It is curious to note that some of the elements required to make a decision require a decision. You must decide at what point you have enough facts. You have to draw some sort of conclusion from the facts. You have to decide what alternatives should be considered. As with most of the material in this book, we can only generalize and take up the most important aspects of the many procedures involved.

Can you recall how we defined leadership? Very simply. To lead is to show the way. If you were to make a list of the many characteristics required of a good supervisor, you could gather most of them under the heading Leadership. A supervisor, by the very nature of his job, has to show others the way. You

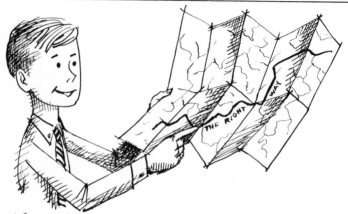

must learn to expect this, and to accept showing the way as a part of your responsibilities. Some of the skills expected of leaders are given in the following list:

Speaking to people as equals
Taking the initiative
Having respect, both for superiors and
    subordinates
Making people feel important
Not showing favoritism
Demonstrating an interest in each individual
Having firmness and determination

The last subject we discussed with you under Supervisory Skills covered honesty. We are not going to dwell upon this here, but merely repeat the three possible definitions for the word honesty:

Not lying, cheating, or stealing
Not hiding one's real nature, being frank and open
Not mixed with something of less value, genuine

You must recognize that being honest as a supervisor goes much deeper than any one of the usual connotations for the word honest.

Everything we have been discussing has been a factor in the task of supervising people. You have heard it said that some people seem to have a knack for directing others. We tell you again, such capabilities simply demonstrate the application of the supervisory skills we have covered in this book. Let's examine some of the points we discussed with you. Listed below are four principles you can apply to achieve good job relations with the folks working for you:

Let each worker know how he is getting along.
Give credit where credit is due.
Tell people in advance about the changes which affect them.
Make the best use of each person's ability.

These principles are the key to dealing successfully with people. To forget them is to lose the key. Don't!

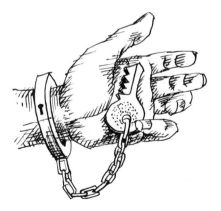

We discussed how people learned. You were told that if people worked for you, you would be required to provide some training. Explaining your position or viewpoint, for example, may be a form of training. It is that simple. When your supervisory tasks require you to teach the worker how to perform or do something, you should remember people learn rapidly in the beginning because they are motivated to learn. As the task becomes harder or more tiresome, motivation tends to taper off and people slow down. The ability to learn seems to lag. You should expect this and try to provide enough variation in your program to counteract this letdown. Try to keep in mind that, whatever the area of training, you should try to explain not only HOW but WHY to the person you are teaching. Knowing the why and wherefore of the job will help the learner avoid mistakes which could disrupt subsequent operations.

It is common knowledge that some people learn faster than others. The faster learner doesn't necessarily learn more, however. You are cautioned against drawing conclusions about people based upon their learning speeds. You could have someone working for you who has had very little formal education. This may be through no fault of his. This person may be handicapped by a lack in reading ability, and yet his capacity to remember and to function with skill may be excellent.

One of the most important functions of a supervisor is to maintain proper communications. While we communicate in many ways, the most common is by talking. You must guard against using terms or jargon which may not be understood by a new employee. When you explain something, take time to find out whether the other person is understanding exactly what you mean. Get some feedback from the person or the group.

Another form of communication is listening. You should train yourself to be a good listener. In this way you can keep abreast of changing situations.

For practically every job we have some measure for performance, whether it has been written down, spoken, or just thought about. In most cases, we have established performance standards for both quantity and quality of work. Using these as a guide, we can tell whether the job is being done as expected, better, or worse. By using job standards, we can determine whether additional training appears to be necessary. We can also use them to provide a firm basis for upgrading outstanding workers.

We trust that you will make good use of all the guides like performance standards and the test materials available from personnel files. We hope, above all, that you will make good use of the concepts and ideas you have learned in these pages. You will find on the following pages a clean copy of the Pre-Test you took at the beginning of the course. Fill in the answers once again. Then you can compare them with the ones you gave when you started and finally, you can check them by turning to the answers at the end of the book.

ABCDE798765432

Pre-Test,
Post-Test,
and
Answers

Pre-Test

(The figures in parentheses show the points to be scored for each correct answer.)

1. Name five basic reasons why people work.

   a._____ (2)

   b._____ (2)

   c._____ (2)

   d._____ (2)

   e._____ (2)

2. People differ in many ways. Can you list three ways other than in appearance and speech?

   a._____ (2)

   b._____ (2)

   c._____ (2)

3. Name three ways people learn.

   a._____ (2)

   b._____ (2)

   c._____ (2)

4. Of all the factors in the learning process, which is considered the most important?

_____ (5)

5. Supervisory skills include getting things done and delegating work. Can you name three others?

    a._____ (3)

    b._____ (3)

    c._____ (3)

6. Briefly, what should a supervisor do to improve his supervisory skills?

_____

_____ (5)

7. In addition to identifying the problem, what are the five steps to making a good decision?

    a._____ (3)

    b._____ (3)

    c._____ (3)

    d._____ (3)

    e._____ (3)

8. What is your definition of leadership?

_____

_____ (5)

9. List two leadership skills.

   a._____ (5)

   b._____ (5)

10. Name three of the recognized principles for creating good job relations.

   a._____ (3)

   b._____ (3)

   c._____ (3)

11. Does a learning curve show how much is learned or at what rate something is learned?

_____

_____ (5)

12. We communicate in many ways. Which is the most common form of communicating on the job?

_____ (5)

13. Would you say job standards can be used to deter-
    mine whether a person needs more training? An-
    swer yes or no._____ (5)

14. You have probably heard it said that safety is
    everybody's business. Given any group of work-
    ers, who would you say should be most responsi-
    ble for their safety?

    _____ (5)

Answers to this test can be found on page 177.

Post-Test

(The figures in parentheses show the points to be scored for each correct answer.)

1. Name five basic reasons why people work.

    a._____ (2)

    b._____ (2)

    c._____ (2)

    d._____ (2)

    e._____ (2)

2. People differ in many ways. Can you list three ways other than in appearance and speech?

    a._____ (2)

    b._____ (2)

    c._____ (2)

3. Name three ways people learn.

    a._____ (2)

    b._____ (2)

    c._____ (2)

4. Of all the factors in the learning process, which is considered the most important?

_____ (5)

5. Supervisory skills include getting things done and delegating work. Can you name three others?

    a._____ (3)

    b._____ (3)

    c._____ (3)

6. Briefly, what should a supervisor do to improve his supervisory skills?

_____

_____ (5)

7. In addition to identifying the problem, what are the five steps to making a good decision?

    a._____ (3)

    b._____ (3)

    c._____ (3)

    d._____ (3)

    e._____ (3)

8. What is your definition of leadership?

_____

_____ (5)

9. List two leadership skills.

   a._____ (5)

   b._____ (5)

10. Name three of the recognized principles for creat-
    ing good job relations.

   a._____ (3)

   b._____ (3)

   c._____ (3)

11. Does a learning curve show how much is learned
    or at what rate something is learned?

_____

_____ (5)

12. We communicate in many ways. Which is the most
    common form of communicating on the job?

_____ (5)

13. Would you say job standards can be used to determine whether a person needs more training? Answer yes or no._____ (5)

14. You have probably heard it said that safety is everybody's business. Given any group of workers, who would you say should be most responsible for their safety?

_____ (5)

Answers to this test can be found on page 177.

Answers

For each correct answer, score the number of points given in parentheses following each question.

1. The basic reasons people work are based on the following needs:

Food	Companionship
Clothing	Desire to be liked
Shelter	Affection
Security	Prestige
Desire to produce	Conformity

2. People differ other than in appearance and speech in these ways:

Ability	Background
Personality	Mentality
Dexterity	Interests

3. These are some of the ways people learn:

   Understanding
   Practice
   Trial and error

4. <u>Understanding</u> is considered the most important ingredient in the learning process.

5. The list of supervisory skills (besides getting things done and delegating work) is as follows:

>   Being self-confident
>   Bringing out the best in people
>   Cooperating
>   Making decisions
>   Training
>   Communicating

6. A supervisor should <u>analyze himself</u> to determine areas for self-improvement in order to develop his supervisory skills.

7. The steps to making a decision after <u>Identifying the problem</u> are:

>   Get the facts.
>   Weigh the facts and evaluate them.
>   Consider the alternatives.
>   Make the decision and act.
>   Follow up, evaluate, revise as necessary.

8. The definition for leadership is <u>showing the way.</u>

9. These are leadership skills:

>   Speaking to people as equals
>   Making people feel important
>   Taking the initiative
>   Having respect, both for superiors and for sub-
>   ordinates
>   Not showing favoritism
>   Demonstrating an interest in each individual
>   Having firmness and determination

10. These are the four recognized principles for good
    job relations:

    Let each worker know how he is getting along.
    Give credit where credit is due.
    Tell people in advance about changes which affect
      them.
    Make the best use of each person's ability.

11. A learning curve shows the <u>rate</u> at which some-
    thing is learned.

12. The most common form of communication on the
    job is <u>talking</u>.

13. Yes, job standards can be used to determine
    whether a person needs more training.

14. Their supervisor.